The Costume Parade

Written by Greg Lang
Illustrated by Mitch Vane

sundance

Billy and Kate sat in the school assembly.
The principal was talking to all the children.
"Our costume parade will be next Friday.
Everyone should make a costume to wear."

"What are you going to wear for the costume parade?" Billy asked his twin sister Kate.
"I'm going to keep it a secret," she told him.
"Me, too!" he answered.

That night, when they got home,
the twins rushed into their bedrooms
to make their costumes.

"What's going on in there?" asked Mom.
"I'm making my costume for the costume
parade at school," said Billy.

4

"What are you doing with the door shut, Kate?" asked Dad.

"I'm making my costume for the costume parade. It's a secret."

5

"Do we have a big, old coat I can use for my costume?" asked Kate.

"Yes, Kate," said her dad.

"There's one in the closet in the hall."

"Mom, do we have any old pants
I can use for my costume?" asked Billy.
"Yes, Billy. There's a pair in the closet
in the hall."

Every day when they came home from school,
Billy and Kate went into their rooms
and worked on their costumes.

On the night before the big costume parade, Billy asked his mom for some big shoes.

Kate asked her mom for some big shoes, too.

Later that night, Billy said, "I'm ready!"

"I am, too," said Kate.

"Can we see you now?" asked Mom and Dad.

"Oh no! It's a secret," they both said.

"We'll show you in the morning."

The next morning, Mom and Dad called out, "Are you ready?"

"Yes! Here we come!"

"Oh no!" they both said.

"You copied me," said Kate angrily.

"No I didn't. You copied me!" said Billy.

"You both must have had the same idea right from the start," said Mom.
"Maybe you should have told each other," said Dad. "What will you do now?"

"I've got an idea!" said Billy.
"I think I know what it is," said Kate.
The twins rushed into Billy's bedroom.

"And the winners for best costume
at the costume parade are . . .
Kate and Billy—the two-headed monster!"